Billy
THE KID

KATHEY DARNELL

Copyright © 2022 by Kathey Darnell.

All rights reserved. No part of this publication may be reproduced, distributed, or transmitted in any form or by any means, including photocopying, recording, or other electronic or mechanical methods, without the prior written permission of the author, except in the case of brief quotations embodied in critical reviews and certain other noncommercial uses permitted by copyright law.

Printed in the United States of America
ISBN 978-1-958434-26-0 (sc)
ISBN 978-1-958434-27-7 (hc)
ISBN 978-1-958434-28-4 (e)

Library of Congress Control Number: 2022911755

2022.07.08

MainSpring Books
5901 W. Century Blvd
Suite 750
Los Angeles, CA, US, 90045

www.mainspringbooks.com

I would like to dedicate this story to my children, Travis and Jesse, and my grandchildren, John Michael, Laila and Callum. A special thanks to "the man from the big white house." Without him, I probably would never have been exposed to fainting goats. He truly loved each and every one.

Also, thank you, Jesse, for acting as my editor and keeping me on track! I know it wasn't easy!!!

Hi! My name is Billy the Kid. I know, I know, there was a famous person named Billy the Kid from the Old West. Well, I can't help it, that's my name. It's not my fault! The man from the big white house gave me the name. He said he was going to call me Billy the Kid. First of all, because I'm a boy and boy goats are sometimes called "billies". Secondly, baby goats are called "kids". So, I'm Billy the Kid. Usually, your mother gives you a name, but you see, my mother wasn't around to name me. She died when I was born. I try not to feel sorry for myself, but sometimes I do.

Since my mother is not around, the man from the big white house comes out to feed me. He feeds me milk out of a bottle and it is really, really good! He brings me milk about four times a day, even during the night, and he always rubs my head. It really feels good when he does that! He must really like me to feed me all the time and rub my head.

None of the other kids get milk from a bottle. They get a little jealous, but they shouldn't...they have mothers to feed them milk.

Besides getting special milk and head rubs, I think the other kids are also jealous because I have a special name. If they knew how sad I felt sometimes, they wouldn't be so jealous. Don't tell anyone, but sometimes when no one can see, or I'm alone, I cry a little bit. After all, I don't have a mother like the other kids, and I have another problem I haven't told you about.

I am the clumsiest kid you have ever seen. I'm so clumsy it's just plain embarrassing! If I fall over, and that's a lot, I can't get up!!! Do you believe it? As if I don't have enough problems! When I do fall over the man from the big white house comes out and helps me get up. Sometimes, if I wait long enough, I can get up by myself.

Why, just the other day, the HUGE dog, Buster, that lives at the house barked at some of us kids and nearly scared me to death and, of course, I just fell over like someone had pushed me. My legs went stiff and straight up in the air. It was awful! Talk about embarrassing! I wish they would get rid of that dog. His bark is really scary. Sometimes I think he barks at me just to see me fall over. Either that or he loves to bark! What kind of name is Buster anyway? Buster??? How did they come up with that name? At least my name makes sense.

Some of the other kids can climb up on anything, things that are almost straight up, but not me. I wish I knew what was wrong with me. Sigh! Maybe if my mother was around, she would know.

What an exciting day this has been! It started early this morning just after the sun came up. One of the mother goats, or "nannies" as people call them, had a baby kid this morning, but it died just after it was born. Everyone was talking about how sad she was, and I knew just how she felt. But here's the exciting part—the talk around the barnyard was that she wants to adopt me. I couldn't believe it! I was so excited I forgot to fall over all morning!

Sure enough, early this afternoon, she came over to me and said, "Hi, Billy...I guess you heard what happened." I said, "I sure did and I'm really sorry. I know you're really sad, like I was when my mother died." She lowered her head and said, "Yes, I am sad and lonely. Are you lonely, Billy?" "Oh, yeah, am I ever! Maybe you'll have another kid real soon so you will feel better." She smiled a little and said, "Well, maybe I will some day, but right now I have another idea. I know you miss your mother and I sure miss my kid, so why don't I be your mother? I know I can't take the place of your real mother, but I think we would be good for each other. I've got all this milk that will go to waste unless I find a nice kid like you to drink it—what do you say?" I was so excited all I could do was nod my head over and over.

"Well, then let's stop all this jabbering on and on, so you can try some real nanny milk." "Does it taste different from the milk in the bottle?" Billy asked. "Oh yes, because this milk was made with love!

Don't drink too much now or you'll get a tummy ache." Then I started drinking—she was right, it was great!

It WAS better than the milk the man from the big white house fed me in the bottle.

I guess she was happy I was enjoying it so much, because she let me drink as much as I wanted and I drank a lot! I drank so much I thought I would burst. She was right again—I did get a little tummy ache, but I didn't care!

After I drank all that milk, I suddenly remembered I hadn't told her about my clumsy problem. I thought, "Oh no, what if she doesn't want to adopt me after I tell her how clumsy I am. She may not want a kid that falls over all the time." I decided I'd better tell her now and get it over with, so I did.

Get this—when I told her about my problem she just started laughing! I was a little angry at first because she laughed at me, but I wasn't angry for long. She said, "Honey, you're not clumsy, you're special. You're part of a breed of goats called fainting goats. It's a very good thing to be. Your mother was a fainting goat. People love to see fainting goats because they are different, not just your ordinary, run-of-the-mill goat like me. People will come from all over just to see you, just like they did your mother." "My mother was a fainting goat too?" "She sure was!" I thought to myself, Wow, things are really looking up."

In one day, my whole life has changed. I have a new mother, who truly wants me, and I know that I'm not just clumsy...I'm special and my real mother was special too. I think I'll strut around the barnyard tomorrow (just a little) and tell everyone I'm not clumsy after all—I'm special!

As night time comes and we snuggle down together in the straw getting ready to go to sleep, I thought how good things have turned out, just when I thought things were really, really bad. Wow...what a great day!!!

Now, if they would just get rid of that crazy dog, Buster!

Even though this story is fictional, the fainting goat species is very real. Marshall County, TN is the first place of known origin in the U.S for this unusual animal and dates back to the 1880's. This species is sometimes called by other names, such as stiff-legged, nervous or wooden leg. Fainting goats can be any color, but some say the original color was black and white, and it is still the most common color today. It is also my favorite.

As the story goes, a man name John Tinsley moved into the northern part of the county bringing with him four goats and a cow. Some sources say the man came from Nova Scotia. His goats were a little different from the typical goat—when startled the goats had a tendency to stiffen or lock up, sometimes losing their balance and falling over. Mt. Tinsley stayed only a short time and when he left he sold or gave his goats to a local doctor. These distinct goats went on to reproduce and thrive in Marshall County. Now they can be found in many countries because of their unique characteristics. Fainting goats are great around kids and make excellent mothers.

Technically, fainting goats have a neuromuscular condition called Myotonia Congentia. This condition causes the animals' muscles to freeze; thus, making them stiffen or fall over. They do not actually faint as the name suggests. Some goats learn to keep on walking very stiffly.

The severity of the symptoms varies from goat to goat. However, it is not harmful in any way—it just makes them special.

CPSIA information can be obtained
at www.ICGtesting.com
Printed in the USA
BVHW090618101222
653837BV00016B/1595